Poli Sci

By Rachel N Stewart

CONTENTS

1. INTRODUCTION

Have you ever wanted to know how and why do we have an American Government? Who were the founding fathers of government? When were some of the policies and procedures put into place that we must follow as citizens? Why will we be placed in jail for violating the law? Do you wish you knew everyday laws and things to better your life?

If so, this book has that covered. It is a simple and easy to understand guide that includes a variety of topics that one should know about American Government. This guide can help anyone navigate through life daily.

This book covers things that I have taught students as a college professor. I am just presenting some of my ideas of what these topics represent. You the reader are at your own free will to add or delete information you see fit to help you navigate on your journey in this thing we call life. This is just a book based off MY logic that I am giving out of love for people and community. Never have I seen a book created on this topic before, so I thought it would be a great idea to put things together in government together.

This book does not cover everything in detail, however if you would like to hire me to speak at a class, conference, or any type of event on the subject matter discussed in this text, I would be more than happy to consult with you and your team. My contact information is at the end of the book.

2. WHY GOVERNMENT IS IMPORTANT?

Government, politics, and policymaking are all important parts of the policy making process in United States government.

Government is the institution with authority to set policy for society. Whereas politics is the way in which decisions for a society are made and considered binding most of the time by most people.

The government affects Americans through regulations, taxes, and services. Government services helps all Americans. Government regulation and services cost money. Government affects the nation's quality of life. Did you know that there is a slight difference between government and politics? Politics is broader than government and competitive. While the distribution of government benefits is a part of the economy and the allocation of their costs.

One act that helps the citizens of the United States is The Americans with Disabilities Act (ADA). The federal law designed this act to end discrimination against persons with disabilities and eliminate barriers to their full participation in American society. The act protects people with disabilities from discrimination in all employment practices, including hiring, firing, promotion, and compensation.

Did you know that the Gross Domestic Product is the value of the goods and services produced by a nation's economy in a year, excluding transactions with foreign countries.

The policymaking process in American government starts with public policy. Public policy is what government chooses to do or not to do about public problems. Some government programs are meant to meet the needs of the public. The policy making process is a logical sequence of activities affecting the development of public policies. The policymaking process has several stages: the agenda setting, policy formulation, policy adoption, policy legitimation, policy implementation, policy evaluation, and policy change.

The agenda setting stage is where the government officials and groups outside of the government compete to determine which problems the government will address. The agenda setting stage addresses the problems of the low wage workers.

The policy formulation is the development of strategies for dealing with the problems on the policy agenda.

The policy adoption process is the official decision of a government body to accept a particular policy and put it into effect.

The policy legitimation process is the actions that are taken by the government officials and others to ensure that most citizens regard a policy as a legal and appropriate government response to a problem.

The policy implementation process is the process in which policies are carried out.

The policy evaluation process completes assessment of policies.

The policy change process is the modification of a policies goals and means considering new information or shifting political environments.

English Influences on American Government

WHAT IS THE AMERICAN SYSTEM?

Delegates turned to their British heritage and adopted many principles of government from England.

Representative Government

Parliament is the law-making body of Great Britain. Parliament is also bicameral (having two houses which can check the work of the other house).

Magna Carta "Great Charter" document that the nobles forced King John to sign. The King's powers were limited. The King also had to obey the laws. The Magna Carta guaranteed that free people could not be arrested, put in prison, or forced to leave their nation unless they were given a trial by jury of their peers. Also, guaranteed that the citizens of England were to be judged according to English Law only. It also protected the rights of Parliament against monarchs.

<u>**English Bill of Rights**</u> Establish freedom from taxation with representation. The right to bear arms. Freedom from cruel and unusual punishment. Maintaining an army during peacetime.

3. IDENTIFY SIGNIFICANT PERSONS AND
    EVENTS

The United States Constitution started
everything for the framing of our country.

PHILOSOPHERS

<u>John Locke</u>: believed the government should
provide natural rights to all citizens. All citizens
should have life, liberty, and property. These are
rights that should not be taken from an
individual and can be called inalienable rights.

<u>Baron de Montesquieu</u>: believed in the
separation of powers with the government, such
as the separation of the church and state.

<u>Niccoli Machiavelli</u>: the inventor of Political
Science and did not revolutionize the study of
government and politics until he turned the age
of 44. He created the book, *The Prince,* and his
intention for writing that book was to make
himself more marketable for gaining in
government.

<u>Jean Jacques Rousseau</u>: believed that the social
contract would be broken and the governed
would be free to choose another set of governors
if the rulers would protect the ruled.

The primary reasons of the Declaration of Independence:

- In 1775, people were angry about new taxes and actions of the British Parliament, the American Delegates from all 13 colonies gathered at Philadelphia.
- The delegates appointed a committee to draw up a Declaration of Independence.
- Thomas Jefferson wrote most of the Declaration of Independence.
- The colonies had officially broken with Great Britain and the war was over.
- July 4, 1776, Congress approved the final draft of the Declaration of Independence.
- John Locke believed that the Declaration of Independence announced the colonies' independence and listed reasons why revolted. It was believed that all men were supposed to be created equal by the creator.

In 1776, the United Stated declared Independence from England and won its independence in 1783. The thirteen original States (New Jersey, Maryland, Virginia, Massachusetts, Rhode Island, Connecticut, New York, Pennsylvania, North Carolina, Georgia, Delaware, South Carolina, and New Hampshire) had rules which were called the Articles of Confederation. Each state was like its own country and had its own set of rules. Each state

had to defend themselves. Delegates from each state sent the leader of their state except Rhode Island. The delegates agreed that the U.S. Government could make rules for all the states. Thus, the birth of the Constitution of the United States.

The Constitution does several things. The Constitution creates a national government for the United States and makes rules for how government work. The Constitution says the government cannot take away certain rights from the people of the United States. The Constitution allows the state governments to keep certain rights and responsibilities.

The Framers for the rules of government were George Washington, James Madison, Alexander Hamilton, and Benjamin Franklin. The Framers created a democratic republic to combine thirteen states under one government. The

Framers who were also called Founders believed that government should make rules for the government and the people which today we call laws. The laws were meant to be obeyed by the people. The Constitution created the branches of government.

The three branches of government help balance the United States government. The three branches of government are the legislative branch, executive branch, and the judicial branch of government. The legislative branch, which is operated by Congress, makes the laws. People elect individuals from each state to represent them. Congress is divided into the House of Representatives and the other is the United States Senate. Congress has the power to make laws about businesses that affect more than one state. Also, Congress has the power to create an army and a navy or other branches of the military. Congress can make laws about taxes.

The executive branch which is led by the President of the United States and is also known as the Commander in Chief. The President carries out the laws Congress makes due to the Constitution. People in this branch make sure people obey laws about business and money.

The President and departments of the cabinet are as follows:

"President-Department of State-Department of Homeland Security-Department of Veterans-Department of the Treasury-Department of Transportation-Department of the Interior-Department of Health and Human Services-Department of Housing and Urban Development-Department of Agriculture-Department of Energy-Department of Labor-Department of Education-Department of Commerce-Department of Justice-Department of Defense"

The President meets with other leaders of other states and countries. The vice president takes the place of the president and is the president of the Senate. The Vice President gets to vote in the Senate when there is a tie.

The Judicial branch or the Supreme Court, states have their own courts. Courts decide to settle disagreements about the law and explain or interpret what the law means. Judges determine in the court of law whether a person has disobeyed the law and how to punish people who have not abided by the law.

The Constitution gives the United States government powers that under the Articles of Confederation did not have. The Constitution is the Supreme Law of the Land. The laws of the United States government take priority over and above the laws of the states.

The separation of powers was created to give some power to only one branch of government. Checks and balances were created to give rules that each branch of power must control the powers of the other branches. A form of checks and balances is veto power. If the president does not sign a law, then that is a veto. If Congress wants to make a law after the president's veto they can. Two-thirds of the members of each house must agree to it. If the law violates the Constitution, then the law cannot be enforced.

The Constitution tells how long government leaders can be in office. The leaders must be elected by the voting population. The leaders in the House of Representatives keep their seat for two years, while the Senate keeps their seat six years. A term is what is called while a candidate or a leader is in office. The president has a four-year term. However, there is no limit on the number of terms for members of Congress. Federal judges serve for as long as they live. The only way the federal judges lose their jobs is through being impeached.

The Founder's of the Constitution created Amendments so things could be changed in the Constitution. Two-thirds of each house of Congress must suggest an amendment. Two-thirds of the state's legislative branch must suggest an amendment. When three quarters of the states agree then an amendment is suggested. The Constitution has been amended 27 times.

After having the Constitution written and the people of the states approved it. Ten amendments were added in which people call the Bill of Rights. The first nine amendments state that the government cannot take away certain rights from the people. The tenth amendment deals with the rights of the states.

THE BILL OF RIGHTS: James Madison proposed the US Bill of Rights

Amendment 1: Freedom of religion, speech, and the press; rights of assembly and petition

Amendment 2: Right to bear arms.

Amendment 3: Housing of soldiers

Amendment 4: Search and arrest warrants

Amendment 5: Rights in criminal cases

Amendment 6: Rights to a fair trial

Amendment 7: Rights in civil cases.

Amendment 8: Bails and fines and punishments

Amendment 9: Rights retained by the people.

Amendment 10: Powers retained by the states and the people.

AMENDMENTS

Amendment 11: Any **state can be sued by a U.S. citizen.**

Amendment 12: Changes in electoral college procedures.

Amendment 13: Abolishes and prohibits slavery.

Amendment 14: Citizenship due process equal protection.

Amendment 15: U.S. cannot prevent a person from voting because of race, color, or creed.

Amendment 16: Congress is given the power to tax incomes.

Amendment 17: The direct election of senators.

Amendment 18: Prohibition of liquor.

Amendment 19: Women gain the right to vote.

Amendment 20: Procedures for outgoing president and the new president coming in.

<u>Amendment 21</u>: Repeal of prohibition (18th Amendment)

<u>Amendment 22</u>: Limit on presidential terms.

<u>Amendment 23</u>: District of Columbia receives electoral votes.

<u>Amendment 24</u>: Prohibits federal and state governments from charging poll tax.

<u>Amendment 25</u>: Presidential succession and presidential disability.

<u>Amendment 26</u>: 18-year-olds gain the right to vote.

<u>Amendment 27</u>: Any change in congressional salaries takes place after the general election.

The **Preamble to the Constitution** is the introduction that explains why the U.S. Constitution was written.

The **Preamble** states: "We the people of the United States to form a more perfect Union establish Justice, ensure domestic tranquility, provide for the common defense, promote the general welfare, and secure the blessings of liberty to ourselves and our posterity, do ordain and establish this Constitution for the United States of America. "

We as United States citizens have a right to choose leaders and lawmakers who will protect our right by voting.

<u>HOW A BILL BECOMES A LAW</u>

1. The bill was introduced in one chamber of Congress. Senate: Stands and reads House: Places in Hopper.
2. The bill is assigned to a standing committee.
3. The standing committee reports the bill back to the floor. (Whole Chamber)
4. The bill is placed on a congressional calendar (the schedule for the debates).
5. The chamber considers the bill-debate is held.
6. A vote is held. If it passes the first chamber, then it is called an act.
7. The Act is sent to the other chamber.
8. The conference committee meets to iron out the difference in the versions of the legislation.
9. The legislation is sent to the President for his signature. The president could veto the legislation.
10. Congress may override a veto by a 2/3's vote of both chambers (becomes law).

What happens in the Federal System?

The federal system is a political system that divides power between a central government with authority over the entire nation and a series of state governments.

The Constitution delegates powers to the national government while leaving other powers to the states.

Delegated powers are granted to the national government.

Legislative power is how laws are made.

The power of the purse is the authority to raise and spend money.

Tariffs are taxes on imported goods.

Congress levies taxes.

Necessary and Proper Clause which gives Congress the power to make all laws.

14th **Amendment**

Expands the authority of Congress.

Due Process Clause that the constitutional provision declares that no state shall "deprive any person of life, liberty, or property, without due process of law."

Equal protection clause: "No state shall…deny any person within its jurisdiction the equal protection of the laws."

EXECUTIVE BRANCH

Enforce laws, to the President, with declaring that the president should "take care that laws be faithfully executed."

The President may make policy recommendations to Congress, receive ambassadors, and convene special.

JUDICIAL BRANCH

Interpret the laws in a Supreme Court and whatever other federal courts Congress sees fit to create.

The Constitution gives the Supreme Court of the United States the authority to try a limited range of cases.

The National Supremacy Clause is where the Constitutional provisions declares that the Constitution and laws of the United States take precedence over the constitutions and laws of the states.

Federal mandates are a legal requirement placed on a state or local government by the national government requiring certain policy actions.

<u>**No Child Left Behind (NCLB)**</u> which is a federal law that requires state government and local school districts to institute basic skills testing as a condition for receiving federal aid.

School Lunch Program is a federal program that provides free or reduced lunch to children from poor families.

LEGISLATIVE BRANCH

This branch of government is made up of the House and Senate, which is known as the Congress.

Separation of powers is the division of political power among executive, legislative, and judicial branches of government.

Role of States in the Federal System

Full Faith and Credit Clause is the constitutional provision.

Defense of Marriage Act (DOMA) federal law stipulating that each state may choose either to recognize or not recognize same sex marriages performed in other states.

Privileges and Immunities Clause is a constitutional provision prohibiting state governments from discriminating against the citizens of other states.

Extradition returns from one state to another for a person accused of a crime.

<u>**Federal System supports**</u>:

Federal Grant Programs, in which the national government gives money to state and local governments to spend in accordance with set standards and conditions.

Block grant programs provide money for programs such as childcare, job training, housing, and workforce training.

The Federal government is mostly awarded and with conditions through formula grants. Formula grants give grant money based on a formula (population, poverty, and overcrowded housing) by Congress.

PUBLIC OPINION

What is public opinion?

A public opinion does not dictate what government officials do so much as it limits the available options.

Public Opinion and Public Policy

A zone of acquiescence is the range of policy options acceptable to the public on a particular issue. The zone changes as does that of the public opinion.

Political Socialization

Political socialization is the process by which individuals acquire political knowledge, attitudes, and beliefs.

Proof of socialization (the more you learn about certain issues your ideologies change) The person who you were ten years ago, and the person who you are today should be a different person. I know things I was against years ago; I have a totally different perspective about it. Never say what you do not think is right or wrong because your view and values will change over time.

How do you measure public opinion?

Public opinion is measured by surveys, random samples, research, and biased samples.

Survey research measure public opinion. People in political campaigns employ polls to plan strategy and find out the main issues that are a concern to the constituents.

A constituent is a person who is represented by an elected official.

Biased sample is an unrepresentative sample that tends to produce results that do not reflect the true characteristics of the universe.

Random sample is an unbiased sample in which each member of a universe has an equal chance of being included.

Political efficacy is the extent to which individuals believe that they can influence the policymaking process.

POLITICAL PHILOSOPHY

Liberalism is the political philosophy that favors the use of government power to foster the development of the individual and promote the welfare of society.

Liberals usually favor government regulation and high levels of government spending for social programs.

Conservatism philosophy that government power undermines the development of the individual and diminishes society. Conservatives believe government regulation and social programs generally do harm rather than good.

Political right (right wing) conservatism

Political left (left wing) liberal

POLITICAL PARTICIPATION

The activity that has the intent or effect of influencing government action (people do not admit the truth) in some instances is what is considered political participation.

Political movement is a group of people that want to convince other citizens to act on issues that are important to the group.

FORMS OF PARTICIPATION

Personal resources: time, money, and civic skills

Psychological Engagement: when people or constituents think they can influence policymaking processes.

Voter Mobilization: setting up random voter registration events to encourage citizens to vote.

Community involvement: canvassing, social media and phone banks (just do not call someone on the Do Not Call: DNC list).

VOTER TURNOUT

Voting Eligible Population (VEP) the number of United States residents who are legally qualified to vote.

Voting Age Population (VAP) the number of United States residents who are 18 years old or older.

People who are psychologically engaged are more likely to vote than people who are not (politically engaged).

Voter turnout is low now because people tend to look for the now of what they can receive now and not the end goal or long-term effects of policies being made by legislation today can affect tomorrow.

PATTERNS OF PARTICIPANTS

(No statistics my views)

Income: A person with a $100,000 a year salary is more than likely to vote than someone who makes minimum wage.

Age: Young adults can change the spectrum if they see the impact voting has on the community and the country as an entire whole.

Race/Ethnicity: More Caucasians vote than any other race or ethnicity.

Gender: Women are more likely to vote, and men are more likely to run for office.

THE NEWS MEDIA

People are getting their news now online and in social media outlets instead of a newspaper like in the old days. You cannot always believe everything you see and read on the internet. Things are most of the time altered with an agenda that is hidden from you but not the person who is coming up with the agenda. This is another story that one day will get told.

<u>TYPES OF OLDER NEWS MEDIA OUTLETS </u>(Veteran Outlets)

<u>Public Broadcasting Service (PBS)</u> a nonprofit private corporation that is jointly owned by hundreds of member television stations throughout the United States.

<u>National Public Radio (NPR)</u> is a nonprofit membership organization of radio stations.

The Corporation for Public Broadcasting is a government agency chartered and funded by the United States government with the goal of promoting public broadcasting.

GOVERNMENT REGULATIONS ON NEWS MEDIA

The freedom of the press is covered in the Constitution in the First Amendment.

The Federal Communications Commission (FCC) regulated the broadcast media using the public airwaves. The Supreme Court allows the FCC to regulate the airwaves. The Fairness Doctrine is an FCC regulation that requires broadcasters to present controversial issues of public importance and to cover them in an honest, equal, and balanced manner.

Shield Law is a statute that protects journalists from being forced to disclose confidential information in a legal proceeding.

COVERING THE NEWS

People who are running for office often try to put candidates in the spotlight that they really want to win who has the most campaign money for press in a positive light.

Most campaign managers will choose a single theme for their clients to be known for during the campaign process. Family is a key focal point, and they like having a person to run that is married with an animal with the so-called American dream lifestyle without scandals. But it normally does not end that way.

A **sound bite** is what is typically created for a candidate's speech and that is what the candidate is known for as a short phrase throughout their campaign.

The media influences policymaking through framing, which is a process by which a communication source, such as a news organization, defines and constructs a political issue or public controversy.

INTEREST GROUPS

What is an interest group?

An interest group is an organization of people who join voluntarily based on some interest they share for the purpose of influencing policy.

Why do people join interest groups?

Most people join interest groups to be with like-minded people with the same morals, culture, and social views.

- Material or monetary benefits
- Solidary or social benefits
- Purposive incentives (expressive incentives: such as working for a cause)

POLITICAL PARTIES

A **political party** is an organization that seeks political power.

The United States of America was created on a two-party system, which is the division of voter loyalty between two major political parties.

The third party is a minor party. I am at this party because I have never solely sided with one party on anything. I believe we should do what is beneficial for the people.

The **Electoral College** is the system established in the Constitution for indirect election of the president and the vice president, it awards electoral votes to candidates that win the most popular votes in a state.

PARTY ORGANIZATION

Democratic National Committee (DNC) raised more money than the Republican Party in 2010, however the Republicans narrowed the gap because they benefitted more than did the Democrats.

Republican National Committee (RNC) also called the GOP (Grand Old Party)

Access is the opportunity to communicate directly with legislators and other government officials in hopes of influencing the details of policy.

REGISTER TO VOTE AND VOTE

National Voter Registration Act (NVRA): passed in 1993 by Congress and President Bill Clinton in which is also known as the Motor Voter Act. It is a federal law designed to make it easier for citizens to register to vote by requiring states to allow mail registration and provide an opportunity for people to register when applying for or renewing drivers' licenses as well as when visiting federal, state, or local agencies, such as welfare offices.

4. **VARIOUS POLITICAL PERSPECTIVES**

Six Goals of Government

1. Form a more perfect union.
2. Establish justice.
3. Ensure domestic tranquility (make Peace within the country)
4. Provide for the common defense.
5. Promote general welfare.
6. Secure the blessings of liberty to ourselves and our posterity.

Purposes of Government

1. Maintain order (make and enforce laws: Constitution was a written plan of government)
2. Public Service (provide essential services to individuals)
3. National Security (protects people from attacks from foreign countries provided by the military)
4. Make Economic Decisions (setting goals making budgets, and cooperating with other governments)

Eight Criteria of Democracy

1. The right to vote.
2. The right to be elected.
3. The right of political leaders to compete for support and votes.
4. Free and fair elections.
5. Freedom of association.
6. Freedom of expression.
7. Alternative sources of information.
8. Institutions for making public policies depend on voices and other expressions of citizens preference.

POLITICAL CULTURE

What is Capitalism?

Capitalism is an economic system characterized by individual and corporate ownership of the means of production, and a market economy based on the supply and demand of goods and services. Also, capitalism can also be called socialism to some, which is an economic system charactered by governmental ownership of the means of production and control of the distribution of goods and services.

What is a mixed economy?

A mixed economy is an economic system that combines private ownership with extensive governmental intervention.

The <u>public sector</u> is a governmentally owned segment of the economy.

The <u>private sector</u> is a privately owned segment of the economy.

What is democracy?

A government ruled by the people.

Types of Democracies:

Direct democracy is in which the people vote & decide on every issue.

Representative democracy is when people give elected officials the power to make laws. This is also called a republic.

Enumerated powers are powers that are given to Congress by the Constitution. Some enumerated powers are levy taxes, borrow money, regulate trade, and coin money.

Constituents are represented by an elected official.

Gerrymandering is a practice of drawing district lines that favor a particular party, politician, or group of people.

What is bicameral and what is its structure?

Bicameral means two houses. The Bicameral Structure consists of the House of Representatives and the Senate. The Founding Fathers divided the Congress into two chambers because they wanted large and small states to be assured representation. The Senate is the upper house, and the House of Representatives is the lower house. Congress has 435 representatives. Every 10 years, after the census is taken Congress determines how the seats in the House are to be distributed. Congress has 100 Senators, which is two per state.

AMERICAN PEOPLE

There is approximately 342 million and counting in the United States. The United States is a melting pot. The country is a superpower and has influence on the actions of the entire world. The Gross Domestic Product is the value of goods and services produced by a nation's economy in a year.

During the Depression, families delayed having children. They thought about how poverty would look with bringing another person in the world. Today, people seem to have children for fun or to save a failing relationship.

The baby boom generation of 1940's and 1950's is a part of the population of Americans that were born after the end of World War II.

HEALTHCARE

<u>Medicare</u> is for people aged 65 and older. America is an aging country and the number the Medicare program helps will grow as the cost of the program.

<u>Medicaid</u> is for persons with low income, such as people with disabilities, the elderly and those who are in true poverty.

<u>Social</u> <u>Security</u> is a federal pension and disability insurance program funded through a payroll tax on workers and their employers.

<u>Health</u> <u>insurance</u> <u>coverage</u> depends on employment or eligibility for government programs.

What is a recession?

A <u>recession</u> is an economic downturn caused by declining economic output and rising unemployment. Currently, the nation has underemployed people. People are taking jobs and not careers now just to survive. A job is totally different than a career. Yet, some are happy to state that jobs are increased for less than survival wages.

A <u>recession</u> is when the United States does not have the fastest growing economy.

What is the Global Economy?

Global economy is the integration of the national economy into a world economic system in which companies compete worldwide for suppliers and markets.

North American Free Trade Agreement is an international treaty that is among the United States, Mexico, and Canada to lower trade barriers among the three nations.

WEALTH, POVERTY, AND HEALTHCARE COVERAGE

The income distribution in America is where the rich get richer. The household income in the United States is based on an individual's race, ethnicity, residence, religion, and gender. The whites and Asian Americans are better off than Latinos and African Americans. The average income is approximately $49,000. Men and women have a gap in education.

POVERTY

What people consider the poverty threshold is the amount of money an individual or an entire family needs to purchase necessities, such as food, clothing, healthcare, shelter, and transportation.

The family size effects the inflation. If a single parent household lack education and skills, they are less likely to be able to support their children.

QUALIFICATIONS AND TERMS FOR ELECTED OFFICES

House of Representatives is at least 25 years old and has been a United States citizen for seven years, legal resident of the state elected from and elected for a two-year term.

Senate must be at least 30 years old, a United States citizen for nine years, a legal resident of state elected and is elected for a six-year term.

All About the Role of the President

The salary of the President is $400,000 a year along with a $50,000 annual expense account, a $100,000 nontaxable travel account and $19,000 for entertainment. The President is elected for four years and cannot exceed two-year terms and ten years. A President shall be 35 years old and a natural born citizen, live in the United States for the last 14 years.

The Electoral College elects the President, and each state has a certain number of electoral votes based on the number of Senators and Representatives in Congress. The popular elections within states determine how the state's electoral votes will be cast. Winners of the populate both are not guaranteed to win the Presidency. The roles of the President consist of represents the country to the world as the Head of

State sees that the laws of Congress are carried out as Chief Executive, proposes legislation as Chief legislator, a party leader, directs foreign policy as Chief Diplomat, and leader of the military.

LANDMARK CASES:

Plessy vs. Ferguson was a separate but equal case.

Brown vs. Board of Education Topeka outlawed segregation in public school and reversed the separate but equal doctrine.

Roe vs. Wade legalized women's right to abortion.

5. KNOW YOUR RIGHTS
THE CRIMINAL JUSTICE SYSTEM

When you get into the "SYSTEM"
- Alleged Crime
- Arrest
- Investigation
- Bail or Detention Hearing

Prosecution and Pretrial
- Formal charges filed.
- Arraignment
- Preliminary Hearing
- Hearings on Defense Motions

Adjudication
- Plea Bargain
- Negotiation
- Trial
- Verdict of Guilty or Not Guilty

Sentencing
- Prison or Probation
- Parole/Supervised Release

What are your Constitutional Rights?

- The right to remain silent. (5th Amendment gives everyone the right not to answer questions by a police officer or government agent.)
- Have an attorney always present before speaking.

- The right to be free from being searched without a warrant or unreasonable searches. (4th Amendment supposed to protect your privacy from government intrusion)

Police cannot search you, your possessions, your home unless:

- You consent (your silence gives police consent)
- Police obtain a search warrant.
- An exception to the search warrant requirement exists.
- Without a warrant, police or government agents may not search your home or office without your consent, and you have the right to refuse to let them in. (State, "I do not consent to this search without my attorney present") Speak out loud and clear so the police will not think you are consenting to them searching your person/property.
- A search warrant is a court permitting a search and seize evidence of a crime. At that time a police officer or can enter your home without permission or your presence.

- <u>Be very respectful when always speaking with authority.</u>
- Exceptions to a warrant are as follows:
- Weapons search within a car or person (wingspan).
- A hot pursuit.
- If evidence is in plain view (doctrine) a cop can legally seize it.
- Patriot Act, intended to get 4th Amendment rights.

<u>The right to advocate for change:</u>

- The First Amendment to the United States Constitution protects the rights of groups and individuals who advocate changes in laws, government practices, and even the form of government.

- There are three kinds of initial police encounters: conversation, detention, and arrest.

<u>HOW TO INTERACT WITH COPS</u>:

- Always keep your hands visible.
- Stay in a well-lit place with witnesses if possible.
- Some cops have on body cameras and dashboard cameras.
- If you plan on recording the police state that you are recording the police. Tell them you are not trying to interfere with an investigation.
- You are under no obligation to converse with the police. If you say anything without an attorney present, you may have whatever you say used against you in the court of law to arrest you or anyone else you speak about.
- Refuse to speak. Make it clear and state that you are refusing to speak. Do not head nod.
- Ask, "Am I being detained? Am I free to go?"

Being detained by a police officer:

- You may <u>only</u> be detained if he or she has a reasonable suspicion that you are involved in a crime.
- There must be more than a reasonable suspicion to arrest someone.
- The reasonable suspicion must be able to be put into words. Placing the suspicion in words makes it an articulable suspicion.
- Ask if you are being detained? Why? Then state you will get an attorney and have your attorney speak on your behalf.

What to do if you are stopped by the police?

- Stay calm and do not be in your emotions.
- Utilize emotional intelligence.
- Avoid arguing with the police but let them know that you know your rights.
- Never run or resist.
- After you have finished speaking with them and ask why you are being stopped. Ask are you free to leave. Provide your id if you are the driver of the vehicle.
- Never ever to consent to a search.
- If you are not free to go, ask why you are being detained.

<u>If you are being detained</u>:

- You must provide your name, address, and date of birth if detained but are not required to say anything else. It is a crime to give a false name. All police must tell you their name, agency, and badge number, along with their police id.
- You may be patted down and any possessions within your reach may be searched if the police suspect you pose a threat of physical injury.
- Write down everything you can remember about the police interaction: police badge number, or name.
- Do not consent to any searches.

Please be aware that the police can lie to you or trick you if they feel like your story is not adding up. They can trick you, but you <u>CANNOT</u> trick them. The law protects the <u>BLUE</u>!

The police will make you promises if you cooperate and tell you that they can lighten your sentence, but what they say is not in writing so please do not believe this and only speak to your attorney.

<u>Am I Under Arrest?</u>

- **The only time a police officer can move you is if you are under arrest.**
- **Do not respond to any police inquiries once you are arrested. Immediately state that your attorney will be speaking on your behalf.**
- **Seek medical attention if you are injured by an officer and take photographs if you are injured.**

If you are arrested, now what?

- The police may arrest you if they witness you breaking the law and have probable cause to believe you have indeed committed a crime or have an arrest warrant that is signed by a judge for your arrest.
- If a police officer arrest you, it is because they witness you doing a non-violent crime.
- When making a arrest this gives the police the right to search you. They may search your bags and may search your vehicle.
- If a officer wants to search your body it has to be an officer of your gender.

<u>YOUR RIGHTS</u>:

State out loud that you want to assert your rights.

"I am going to only speak to my attorney and my attorney will speak on my behalf."

This statement upholds your 5th Amendment right which protects you from police interrogation. Police are not to ask you anymore questions after the statement.

Having an attorney present is your right.

<u>Miranda Rights</u>:

- You have the right to remain silent and to refuse to answer questions.
- Anything you do say can and will be used against you in a court of law.
- You have the right to be an attorney, and to have an attorney present when questioned.
- If you cannot afford an attorney, one will be appointed to you at no charge.
- If you decide to answer questions now, without an attorney present, you will retain the right to stop answering at any time until you talk to an attorney.
- Do you understand these rights as explained to you?
- Knowing and understanding your rights as I have explained them to you, are you willing to answer my questions without an attorney present?

Things you should say when you are demanding your rights:

- I will not talk to you or anyone about anything.
- I demand to have an attorney present before I speak to you or anyone.
- I will not answer any questions, or reply to any charges, without my attorney present.
- I do not agree to perform any test, consent to any searches, or participate in any line ups, except DUI tests that do not involve words.
- I will not sign anything unless my attorney agrees I should do so, except jail release agreement.
- I will not waive any of my constitutional rights.

What is a Grand Jury?

- A grand jury is where someone is subpoenaed in a written order for a person to appear at a secret court proceeding and testify under oath about information the government thinks you may know about a crime or a fugitive.
- You should only speak to your attorney and not any agents until your attorney is present with you. The authorities may try to threaten you, however, do not let them intimidate you.

What are your rights at airports?

- When you buy a ticket, you give airport personnel permission to scan you and your bags and go to the airport. They can do additional random searches of people and their property regardless of whether the initial scan turns up anything suspicious.
- Do not have any weapons in your belongings when going to the airport.
- The pilot on the airplane can refuse to fly a passenger if they believe the passenger is a threat to the safety of the flight.
- If you are from another country, the United States Customs can stop and search you.
- If you are at the border of the country within 500 miles, your rights are reduced.

What is racial profiling?

Is the practice of a police officer targeting individuals as suspected criminals based on their race or ethnicity.

LIST OF PRESIDENTS

1. George Washington
2. John Adams
3. Thomas Jefferson
4. James Madison
5. James Monroe
6. John Quincy Adams
7. Andrew Jackson
8. Martin Van Buren
9. William Henry Harrison
10. John Tyler
11. James K. Polk
12. Zachary Taylor
13. Millard Fillmore
14. Franklin Pierce
15. James Buchanan
16. Abraham Lincoln

17. Andrew Johnson
18. Ulysses S. Grant
19. Rutherford Birchard Hayes
20.James A. Garfield
21. Chester A. Arthur
22. Grover Cleveland
23. Benjamin Harrison
24. Grover Cleveland
25. William McKinley
26. Theodore Roosevelt
27. William H. Taft
28. Woodrow Wilson
29. Warren G. Harding
30. Calvin Coolidge
31. Herbert Hoover
32. Franklin D. Roosevelt
33. Harry S. Truman
34. Dwight D. Eisenhower
35. John F. Kennedy
36. Lyndon B. Johnson
37. Richard M. Nixon
38. Gerald R. Ford
39. Jimmy Carter
40. Ronald Reagan

41. George Bush
42. Bill Clinton
43. George W. Bush
44. Barack Obama
45. Donald J. Trump
46. Joseph R. Biden

VOTE EVERY ELECTION

LET YOUR VOICE BE HEARD

THROUGH

THE POWER OF YOUR VOTE

DO NOT BE SILENCED

YOU MATTER

YOUR VOTE MATTERS

ABOUT
RACHEL N STEWART

Rachel is a graduate of Southern University Baton Rouge Campus with a Bachelor of Arts in History and a Master of Arts in Social Science with a concentration in Political Science. Rachel loves history, politics, real estate, and astrology. She considers herself a lifelong learner, loyal and honest. Rachel has a specialization in real estate of listing homes and helping military families find their new homes and sell their existing property. Rachel is a certified Military Relocation Professional Specialist (MRP) and can help you relocate anywhere in the United States. She has been licensed in the state of Louisiana since 2017 and a member of the National Association of Realtors, Louisiana Association of Realtors, and Realtor Association of Acadiana (RAA). She can help you with property in any of these areas as well as if you need to relocate around the world with the referral partners with Latter & Blum.

Prior to becoming a real estate professional, Rachel was a high school business education teacher for five years where she earned specializations to teach and proctor exams for the following: Customer Service and Sales, Business of Retail, Entrepreneurship and Sales, OSHA training, Diversity, Equity, and Inclusion; Interpersonal Communication Techniques and Microsoft Office (Word, PowerPoint, and Excel). Outside of real estate, Rachel teaches Diversity, Equity and Inclusion, American Government, and International Relations, as a college instructor. Also, she hosts professional development seminars. Rachel's goal in the process of any transaction is to educate you along the way while providing you with excellent customer service.

For all your real estate needs please contact:

Rachel N Stewart, Military Relocation
Professional
REALTOR®
Latter & Blum
Text: 225-803-8704
Office: 337-233-9700
Fax: 337-456-2066
Rachel.Stewart@latterblum.com
www.rachelstewart.latter-blum.com
2000 Kaliste Saloom Road Suite 101
Lafayette, LA 70508
Licensed in the State of Louisiana and
by the LREC

I can help you relocate anywhere in the
World with my referral partners.
Ask me how?

Follow me on YouTube and TikTok
at @IamPolisci

Connect outside of real estate:
InfoForRachel@gmail.com

RNS
RACHEL N STEWART